For Father Da...

Happy Easter an...

from

Angie S?oor
Green Park Home

IT IS I WHO SPEAK:
SELECTED POEMS

It Is I Who Speak:

Selected Poems

NIGEL GERRANS

edited by
FELIX HODCROFT

Valley Press

First published in 2015 by Valley Press
Woodend, The Crescent, Scarborough, YO11 2PW
www.valleypressuk.com

First edition, first printing (February 2015)

ISBN 978-1-908853-51-6
Cat. no. VP0074

Printed and bound in Great Britain by
Imprint Digital, Upton Pyne, Exeter

www.valleypressuk.com/authors/nigelgerrans

Contents

Introduction

Posterity will judge whether a writer's work is fresh, striking and profound enough to deserve re-reading. There may, however, be a problem about that work being available to read in the first place. In the version of capitalism that drives the British poetry world, fashion and connections continue to play a major part in deciding who and what gets published. This means that it can be a salutary exercise to compare, in due course, the selected works of a poet who is or has been prominent with those of a poet who has endured (or even benefited from) relative or complete obscurity. Which of these, as the years pass, is truly the fresher, more striking and profound?

This volume has been prepared in an attempt to ensure that the poems of Nigel Gerrans are not lost to view when such judgements are weighed. Gerrans is one of several impressive modern British poets whose poetic career stretches over many years, who have ranged across a variety of styles and forms and who have, by chance or design, escaped the poetry world's version of 'the mainstream'.

Gerrans was born in 1931 and worked, amongst other jobs, in industry, in teaching and as a hospital chaplain. He wrote poetry from adolescence until severely disabled by a stroke in 2010. He has seen himself – and been seen by the select band of his admirers – as a 'religious' poet, but I think this does him an injustice. Though matters of faith and doubt are recurrent themes, so are the turbulence of the times he has lived through, personal upheavals and the lives of those who have touched him. Meanwhile, in 'Song Sequence', with which this selection closes, he draws together work done over a fifty-five year period, inter-weaving spiritual and lyrical, religious, personal and erotic.

Although the poems in the first section of this selection fall into a rough chronological order, I have ordered Gerrans' work loosely by its themes (though of course these overlap) rather than by date of composition. The first and earliest poem, 'Night Express', dates from 1948; the most recent revisions to 'Song Sequence' were made in 2008-9.

For their help in making this selection from the poems of Nigel Gerrans, I'm very grateful to Joyce Bell, Catharine Boddy, Paul Hughes, Rosie Larner and Jamie McGarry. The final selection is mine, as are decisions made, in a number of these poems, regarding which version or variant reading of a poem to use. I have discussed and debated the form and content of this selection at every stage with Nigel Gerrans himself but the final selection, and the remarks in this introduction, are my responsibility alone.

Felix Hodcroft
Scarborough
June 2014

for Barbara Gerrans,
in appreciation

1.

*"We could never quite find the exact shape,
Fit limb to limb, or life to life succinctly"*

Night Express

Don't talk to me of sleeping sky,
Of dozing stars,
Of red-eyed bleary sunrise.
Give me the alarm shriek in the night,
Give me the whites turning,
The greens and reds twisting,
The blink of startled lights
In a dazzled night.
Give me the speeding
Caterpillar
That eats steel,
That sparks stars,
Fumes flaming smoke
And screams
Against the night.

Hitch-Hikers

'It's not so difficult in pairs,' Jacob said,
When we'd been hauled aboard by those already there
To sit centrally. It was a thirty-footer, bare and
Studded with greasepools sticky under a surface of dust –
And so we came to Exeter.

It was mid-May and had rained,
The grass smelt fresh along the roadside.
A little Austin picked us up when we were a mile or so out,
Just as it was growing dark, the tree branches
Reaching out, black on the sky.
A photographer; he could take us only
To Honiton, but to hop in and welcome.
He'd been in the Army himself, tried hitching a good deal in
    his time.

We had three days in front of us and could afford the luxury
Of taking time, even in the act of getting home –
To sit in cars and talk to photographers about lenses
And lose ourselves in glorious uncharted wastes beyond
    timetables.

Now it was dark. He left us just through Honiton,
Still on the main road. It was nearly ten.
Hedges struck out at us as we walked on the road edge;
The air held the damp mustiness of a country night with
    beetles about.
If we thought of the train, it was only for a moment
When we heard it scream in the distant town.

We passed through a drift of woodsmoke. The photographer
Would be sipping hot coffee. A car passed, then a lorry,
Then nothing for seemingly a very long while.

I was ready to walk the night to its end, was part of the
    dark air.
Our bodies were cool shells cupping the crystalline, fluid
    night,
As it flowed and overflowed about us.
This time a lorry stopped, a furniture van returning empty.
We had it to ourselves as far as Yeovil, and then
We hauled in two other servicemen doing their two years
    like us.
And we all leaned over the tailboard and talked
At the giddy receding void behind, and at the violent light
Of cars as they overtook us, till we'd exhausted ourselves,
And solved most of the earth's problems, and probably
Some celestial ones as well. And then,
Most exquisite pleasure of all, we rolled ourselves back
Into the mounding acreage of felt and sacks,
Breathing deeply of fumes filtering through the flooring,
To loosen our collars and sleep.

And I knew nothing till I saw the dawn sky
With a looped rope from the van roof
Swinging jazzily against it.
By then we were on the white concrete strips
Leading into London and making speed.

Gift

1.

If then I said I loved you it was not so;
I do not know how deep I was in my own slag-sleep,
Can never recall the dream detail,
Am left only with the taste of it, sickening with me,
Acrid, staining, nullifying.

If I said then I loved you it was not so,
I was too deep in that sulphurous sleep,
Given to the city's concentrate night,
Eroded by the alchemy that swells yellow the surface bricks,
Their fungoid growths rotting into my will.

Grey night smoked in my brain;
I was steeped deep in the fog-fumed life.
If I said I loved you then
It was not so;
My need was all I could offer you.

2.

All my love is scattered with the dandelion head;
And I, dry, tatter in the wind
And waste and wait for a word's return
From them for me.

I would see them held in a warm, damp ground,
Or gripping even at brick. But I feel them,
I fear them wind-scratching at a trodden earth,
Or in the ordered garden torn out.
I feel them shrivel into the dust like my stalk,
And my dead head.

3.

All my love is scattered like a broken necklace,
Fled into corners, under floor, under foot;
Its purpose and form spilling out,
Each bead seeded away to a separate silence.

I must string tight a chain again,
I am too many, we are one.
I must string tight the chain again for you,
From me to you.

Memorandum

I am turning to paper, activated now
By the dry spirit desiccating my flesh;
Duplicating, diluting my intention
I sit in the controlled environment
Blanched and flaking, fed by carbons and sometimes
A top copy lending variety, even authority.
I do not hear any longer the background pulse
Of machinery more vital than myself,
It is built into my day/night pattern.
I do not hear and cannot listen,
A necrotic area increasingly unstimulated.
The packaged meal on the disposable cardboard plate
I cannot taste or smell,
But I know and trust its uniformity.
When I move my hand for work reasons
I feel it crackle and see
A dehydrated, cellulose thing.

Monologue

1.

Now all is settled between us satisfactorily.

We could never quite find the exact shape,
Fit limb to limb, or life to life succinctly
While we were together. He did not,
Could not give from himself, there was always
Something he left close-wrapped inwardly.
I tried to learn to accept this,
But could never cease to believe
That love should be outflowing,
Generous; his tightness of soul
Was beyond my understanding.

But I have since come through this door, you see,
And known all from before, and all afterwards;
Now you are welcome. He had taken me, you understand,
Out of his weakness, out of his need, and never gave me,
Was never able to give me, what I asked.
He drained me to the ultimate kiss and caring,
Then returned within his carapace,
Leaving me with my anger,
And two children to train.

And then this happened to me – and to him,
For we were implicit in each other
Whether he acknowledged it or not –
He who would lead his mind's lovers,
Gratuitously,

On his salt-whipped white horses.
No, I am not bitter.
Not any longer.
I know that was essential for him,
Just as I was in my way;
Yet I could not give him
All he needed, only a part;
And that I gave in full.

2.

Now I know how he opened the wardrobes
And clung into my clothes shouting 'I am alone.'
I think he learned to feel some pity then
For my frequent past despair;
Or some remorse for all our time together wasted;
Although for the greater part it was
This awareness of his own sudden isolation
That distressed him most.
And he came every evening
To sit with me.
He who had never been a stayer
Did not miss one visit during those long weeks.
He rubbed cream into my dry-skinned hands
For the sake of something to do.
He brought along in the bright Italian bag
My clean nightdress,
Which he had washed with too much Dreft.
And we sorted out a few matters together,
Between ourselves, in preparation,
Calmly but urgently.

Yes, by the end
We had settled everything between us –
There was no more bitterness –
In that public ward,
During the official visiting hours,
With other people's visitors
Dropping in and leaving all the time,
Clustering round the beds.
'Semper fidelis,' I said to him
Blocking the tracheostomy tube

With the index of my good hand, to make sound.
And all that time we played the double-bluff;
He telling me what the doctors had told him
To tell me;
I pretending
I did not know what was happening to me.

3.

By the end we had settled matters between us,
And I had him to myself
As never once before.
Sometimes he rested his head against my shoulder,
Not too heavily, not to impede my breathing;
I could not talk any more by then,
And we had said everything.
But I wanted to say 'Take me home, take me home,
Please take me away, see the doctor and ask,
For a weekend, a day, for an hour or two.
I can get better there, with just you, on our own.'
I did not want to die in that place,
Surrounded by people who sniggered
When I could no longer hold in my bladder,
The nurses scolding
When I stained their polished floor.
He had offered to speak to the Sister and explain
That I always tried to attract attention in time,
And that no one in the ward could understand me,
But I did not want to create difficulties.
I heard him, you know, that last time;
I knew he was there.
They told him I was in a coma
And could no longer breathe unaided.
The sight of me shocked him
When he came round the curtain
Unreal from the night streets.
I was flushed with the oxygen,
The machine jerked and clicked,
And my breast rose and fell
Mechanically.

4.

He thought I was more beautiful
Than he had ever seen me before,
Even with my eyes staring
Without reason in them.
I knew he was there.
I felt him grab my hand awkwardly,
And he was cold;
And all he said: 'My dove, my dove, oh my little dove.'
And he thought: *Now I am alone.*
Now I am really alone.
I knew all that, and I felt
His lips and his hair and his tears
On my arm. I knew all that then, or perhaps
I knew it when I came through this door; and about
His endless questions on his rounds of the doctors,
His visits to the almoner, to the National Insurance Offices,
To the children parked in various places.
He had brought me photos of the baby I had not held
To cheer me up, and bottles of Whitbread as a treat
For them to pour down my tube, and which I could not taste.

Now you are welcome.
All is settled between him and me.
Satisfactorily.
He has chosen you too out of his weakness,
That I know;
But he may have learnt a little.

A Visit to the Art Gallery

after C.P. Cavafy

As we went in
You were sitting at your table
By the door,
Almost enclosed
By postcards, illustrated catalogues
And pamphlets.

You stamped my ticket
In your machine
And handed it to me
With a polite
And impersonal smile.
I spoke a few
Inconsequential words
To try to stretch the moment.
You smiled again,
And I followed Michael
Into the first viewing room.

You were no longer there
When we left an hour later.
And as Michael talked,
I marvelled once again
That I was not finding
An excuse to wait behind –
It was nearly closing time –
Until you came out.

But would I this time
Have allowed myself
To say, to do
What my hunger
Has always demanded?

The pass
Does not contain
Your writing.
Only your touch.

And now the train draws out,
Leaving you all
Moving away
Along the platform,
Not even waving.

I suppose I was,
Once again,
Paralysed
By the power
Of your beauty.

Impasse

So I do not speak your language,
I do not know your word,
And to you my simple pleading
Is wretched and absurd.
Words will not carry meaning,
Words will not bare the heart,
They only send me reeling
Back to a giddy start.

How can I tell my story,
How can I plead my cause?
My soul's articulation
Does not obey your laws.
There is no time for greeting,
There is no place to be
Where we can hold each other
And stay awhile to see.

The pieces will not gather,
They scatter wider still,
For such a vital movement
I have no art or skill.
My purpose has no power,
It leaches to the drain,
The meaning I have cherished
Leaves but a fading stain.

So the beauty of my longing
Is withered by your heat,
You have no hand to touch me,
We have no place to meet.

From a Photo of My Mother's Grave

It is only a photograph
Sent by the kindly people
Who had visited, on their holiday,
And sought you out.
Now it stands on my desk;
But I have never visited
These sixty years.

Should I now desire
To tear at that compacted earth
With my fingers;
Try to touch a frame
That had structured the woman
Who nursed, fed, caressed me,
Unaware of an ending
So imminent at that time?

Could I now put my hand
In the cavity which held
The womb where I lay curled,
Nurtured all those months;
Touch the cage upon which
I lay to suckle,
Secure, serene?

And after me another foetus
Formed in that same space,
To stir and stretch,
To exult and prepare
For life – abruptly
To be denied.

Two journeys then aborted;
And mine, not long begun,
Distorted by the ensuing travel.
And yet, perhaps, this course
I chose?

They talk of heaven and hell,
Well, let that be;
We cannot tell.
But purgatory –
There they may have a point;
Not later, at some shadowed
Staging post,
But in the harsh
And challenged present –
Purgatory now.

In this I find some ease;
The present time a place
For making souls;
Arena for choice;
Womb in which
To stir and stretch,
To exult and prepare
For life.

The reward must be alone
In this progressive moving;
The task, to find a wisdom
Sufficient only
For the next outreaching.

Woman,
You speak to me,
But silently,
Of courage, purpose,
Meaning,
From a further place
You found.

Stranger

Many of us
Somehow manage
To defer examining
The full effect of our guilts,
The total consequence
Of our imperfections,
Indefinitely.
So where do we find
The courage
Consistently
To sustain
Such a costly
Avoidance?

Are we so intent
On being
Sole author of the life
We have meticulously
Constructed?

Can we dare
To wait
Until a final moment
Forces us
To face the stranger
We never allowed ourselves
To visit?

That will, after all,
Require
A different order
Of courage.

Recessional

The experiments of Time are done,
And lessons learnt, a few;
Now I have to come to hold at last
What perhaps I always knew.
It has taken a weary struggle
To climb the prison wall,
Not to reject who I really am,
But hear the inner call.
Much has been misused, much spoiled,
And many hurts remain,
But the hour has come to sift the gold,
To weigh the loss and gain;
Rejoice in the beauty I can know
And praise through my delight,
Worship from the truth of me
Trusting it shall be right;
Bless with all my keenest sense,
Some of the wonder tell,
To leave a touch of loveliness,
And know all shall be well.

2.

"I'm here you know.
Not just a lump of meat.
Connect. Try looking
Into my eyes."

The Ballad of Ted and Joan

I will tell you the life of Ted and Joan
Who live near Letford junction;
Letford, you know, is a 'village',
A suburb of quiet distinction.

It's really the perfect neighbourhood,
They'd not leave at any price;
So near the shops and so near the town,
Very convenient – so nice!

Of course, they had found it strange at first
But they soon fell in with tradition;
The wash on a Monday, a bonfire on Sunday
And soon they achieved recognition.

Their house is modest and homely,
Like a Tudor cottage – unthatched,
Half-timbered – to match the neighbourhood,
Stuccoed and semi-detached.

Their house and their garden are bordered in front
With a low, neat and squarely-cut privet,
Which invites you to gaze at their life indoors,
To study the way that they live it.

Ted gets up at half past six
And he makes two cups of tea,
Then he chants in the bath till a quarter past seven,
No merrier man than he.

And Joan prepares the breakfast
Of cereal, marmalade, toast,
Then Ted he reads the Chronicle
While Joan she reads the Post.

With a master's perfection of timing,
He rises, bestows one kiss,
Picks up his briefcase and briskly walks out
For the train he could never miss.

But the evenings – ah, the evenings!
Clad in homely attire,
They spend from seven to half past eleven
In front of the living room fire,

Save on Wednesday they go their separate ways,
Ted to the Crown to be witty
While Joan goes down to Mrs Brown's
For a meeting of her Committee.

And on Friday they go to the pictures
To live three hours in a dream,
They sit at the back of the one and nines
In the dark of the Rex or the Queen.

Ted works Saturday mornings
But is back in time for his meal,
'Lovely dear!', then there's the washing-up
And tomorrow's potatoes to peel.

He must polish the car for tomorrow
And then it's time for tea.
He's nearly dead is husband Ted,
No busier man than he.

In the evening there's the wireless
And the Kettlebys from next door;
But the wireless is so much the same as ever
And so is Madge K – the bore!

But Sunday, joint in the oven,
They proceed in state down the street;
They smile and wave recognition,
So many good friends to greet.

Then they sit in their usual pew and pray
That life will go on in the usual way
And they watch the parson raise his hand
In blessing and think that they understand.

Then it's out in the Ford to see the world
To get out – get away from home
In a queue of cars crawling up the road
All trying to be alone.

On Sunday night, as Ted shuts the door
And locks the world out of their life,
He glances up at the sky, at a star,
Then goes slowly back in to his wife.

And as Joan opens the wardrobe,
She sees all her clothes empty there,
She looks at herself in the mirror
And quietly stops brushing her hair.

She stares for a moment, she wonders,
She thinks of their being dead,
Of her mother, his father, his sister,
And turns silently to Ted

And clings to him so close, so tight
To try to dispel the creep of night,
'I should die, Ted, I should surely die too
If anything ever should happen to you!'

And both of them know at that instant
The reason, the point of their life –
That Ted should be her husband,
That Joan should be his wife,

That, clinging to the familiar things
In life, they would surely stay,
Not lose themselves in the mighty river
That is sweeping all away.

Only ripples from that great river
Could lap against them here,
They might even start a family –
In one, maybe two more years.

But nothing too strange or too different
As they both – placid, safe, slightly fat –
Kneel down at Church every Sunday
And ask God to keep it at that.

And they both know that He will attend to it,
For God is a very old friend
And they have no fears at meeting Him
When their lives have wound to an end.

For Joan knows, as she looks in her mirror
And Ted as he turns the front latch,
That God has prepared a cottage for them,
Mock-Tudor and semi-detached.

Bluebell

She has her locker just on the left as you go into the junk
    store.
In the afternoon at three-thirty you will see her – there is
    no door –
Extricating an old green overcoat
From among her brooms and tins of polish,
Taking a mirror from a top shelf to adjust her hat
And tuck away the stray greying hairs;
Last of all she changes her shoes.
I expect the pattern repeats itself in the reverse order
At seven in the morning when she arrives;
But we are never there to confirm this.
Our first sight of her each day
Is at half a minute to nine o'clock
When she takes up her supreme daily task;
One hand on hip, the other cutting wildly at air, cheeks
    flaring,
Dorcas cap askew, green-striped apron glaring impatience,
She stands at the end of the long alley leading to the main
    gate,
Just by the time-punch, exhorting us, who leave only this
    thin margin of time
To slip our card into the clock.
Like an ageless and benevolent goddess
Descending daily at this half-minute of our need,
She gathers her children in, and would not see us lose to
    time,
She who has ruled her world for two silent hours with
    broom and duster.

This duty complete, she will stay modestly among us,
Fetching away our dirty tea-cups, patching the mill-men's
overalls,
Lending a hand in the canteen until three-thirty.
Then she changes her shoes to bustle away down the long
alley
Along the river-walk, and over the bridge to the shops in
Barnes.

Fred

We never said goodnight properly to Fred.
We'd all had a good day at the sports;
But he had not been so self-possessed
As usual after he'd tripped in the sack race
And given up.
That night, he would not apologise for
Making a noise after bed time.

We never said goodnight properly to Fred.
Everyone had enjoyed the zoo but why,
He sneered, should he be grateful?
It was his right to be taken out to the
Cinema, the seaside, to London,
Like other children were.
Yet he wasn't other children.
Hadn't really been a child for a while.
We stayed up with him till eleven thirty but
Still 'I'm free and nobody bosses me!
You're not my mother or Dad and I'm glad
I belong to myself and to nobody else.
Not to this concentration camp!'

Yes. The Charity to him was
So much barbed wire,
He paced his concrete soul.
So much had happened to all of them.
Stuff they could not tell nor understand
And that we should never know.
We tried to pay the unknown debt
Out of our pity's shallow coin but
Could never meet the price.

The song of the children is sad and short and half-expressed.

Mrs Kaeser's song was sad too, but soft.
And David and Lawrence loved it and tried it,
Although they said they did not like singing
And could not understand the words which were German.
Mrs Kaeser was Swiss like the rolls on Thursdays.
She sang to them while they had their bath,
But did not bath them, for they asked me to ask her not to;
She just inspected their ears and teeth and necks afterwards.
Her song was sad too, but soft,
And told much of her gentleness,
And there was warmth in the room, and the smell of clean
    towels,
And steam and soap;
And there was love in the room as she sang,
With her head down over her sewing.

The song of the children was sad and short and half-
    expressed.
Now I want to stay with you.
To stay.
There was Brian who loved swings and see-saws,
Delicate face, he weighed a feather
And swung upside down on your hand like a monkey
Saying 'I like you, don't I, uncle?'
And tiny Barbara, darkness deep in her eyes
Full of wondering and wonder, beautiful to watch.
What of her in ten years time?
What of Terry who had smoked since he was six?
You could see the blue streaks of vein
Under the skin of his cheeks.

What of Susie who held her breath and went purple
rather than go out walking;
Of Carol who asked me to be her father
Till hers came out of prison;
Jane, who helped with everything.
Mike, who said 'I'm going home tomorrow'
And who wasn't.

Why be a child to be weak and stupid,
Believe lies, not be able to tell them yourself
Without giving yourself away?
Child to be bawled at, bossed, ignored,
Why be a child and be soft?
Fred jeered at anything soft,
Prayers and poems and love and
Anything he couldn't understand and
Anyone who wasn't a man;
Jeered at the other kids when they began
With their 'hope I'm dry tonight, sir!'
Or their 'take me home, sir please and
Let me stay
With you!'

There were so many toys there.
It was no good, though.
There were so many broken homes.
Lucky we could blame so much on the war
For the first few years, at least.

We never said goodnight to Fred.

He Still Gets Up at Quarter to Five

I dropped off again
In the intercessions, Father.
Hope I didn't snore. Truth is
I was up, yet again,
Most of the night with the pains.
Walking up and down I was,
Or sitting on the edge of the bed,
Trying not to wake Jack –
Though he's mostly deep gone.
I only got about half an hour;
Had just dozed off when Jack woke up.

He's been retired over sixteen years
But he still gets up at quarter to five,
Makes his cup of tea, and burns his toast.
It's only lately I've managed
To stop him getting the hoover out –
On account of the neighbours.

He was a dockyard worker, you know.
And when he retired, after his fifty-one years,
They hired the steam train,
With the Pullmans,
And took him and his mates –
About ninety in all –
For a five course meal with all the trimmings.
They consumed – if you can believe it –
Two hundred bottles of wine –
He didn't mention the beer –
And the whole thing cost over five thousand.

To and fro twice they went.

Goods Inwards

Before the splash of thin April sunlight can evaporate,
He emerges from his one-bulb hollow
Where he keeps a dangerous single-bar electric fire
On an upturned tin.
He presents his round red face to the light
And blinks for a moment,
Rubbing the eyes under whiskery ginger brows,
Perhaps from the glare, perhaps from relief of tedium.
Then he leans his bulk against the door jamb,
One hand in brown overall pocket,
The other with a finger hooked onto the pipe in his mouth.
He turns his head this way and that,
Like a bird,
His mind hopping from one memory to another,
While the crimson fork-lift trucks
Move about the yard.
Behind him, and down the steps,
Is his office – a magpie store
Papered with cuttings from boxing magazines,
Coloured posters of regimental uniforms,
Crude caricatures of friends,
And the odd cartoon cut from Sunday papers.
He turns his head again from side to side,
Pecking at thoughts,
And waits for the next lorry to draw in.

Lamentation of Patient X

Sometimes I go on a bender you see,
Two or three times a week,
If I can find the cash.
I leave the twins with a neighbour upstairs,
I reckon I'm owed a bit of life
At nearly eighteen, don't you?
Then this van comes from nowhere,
And there I was with both legs shattered,
Bent over my shoulders.

The harvest is over,
The summer is ended,
And we are not saved.

I don't remember much
After the first bleeding pain;
Twenty minutes they were coming,
Me drifting in and out.
Came to, briefly, in Accidents.
Must have been one of fifty or more
That night, druggies included,
Giving the staff hassle;
And some violent.

Is it nothing to you,
All you who pass by?

The dead-eyed doctor
With the hard-drinking face
Was efficient, faultless really,
But speaking
Like something had died inside of him.

'No moral landscape these girls,
No moral subtext,'
He said to the nurse –
Whatever that was supposed to mean.

Is there no balm in Gilead,
No physician there?

Very good at looking into my eyes
With your torch, aren't you, I thought,
And talking over the top of me.
I'm here, you know,
Not just a lump of meat.
Connect. Try looking
Into my eyes
With your eyes,
Doctor!

Behold and see
If there be any sorrow
Like unto my sorrow
Which is done unto me.

Four hours on the slab they said.
Nurses had to do everything for weeks.
I can walk a step or two now.
That's what hospitals are for aren't they.
It's all free and stuff.
What's grateful got to do with anything?

Is there no balm in Gilead?

And then this woman had the bloody cheek to ask –
After everything I've been through, can you imagine –
If I thought I'd paid a high price
For all that booze!

The harvest is over.

High price?
I'd only spent twenty quid
AND got a free taxi ride!

The summer is ended
And we are not saved.

Stupid cow.

To a Woman with a Disfigured Face

You bear your disfigurement
With resignation after all these years,
And with dignity –
No longer the eight-year-old who shouted:
'If they can't do something for me
I am finished.'

You have to bear the half-glances of men,
The stare of the insensitive,
The mirror's confrontation
Each predictable morning.

And there are some
Who have to seek a dignity
Another way.

They bear their particular disfigurement
With resignation, in a secret womb
All their years –
Like some unadmitted pregnancy
That never comes to term.

Perhaps they want to shout
Something.

At Her Own Pace

They come in the gate together,
She checking her still vigorous stride
To his pace.
Indeed she checks her life now
To his pace.

They will have made their way
Down the steep cliff path
Tentatively, as far as the rock pools,
For that is always where he likes to go;
And she has escorted him, not holding hands,
But being there, always alongside.

As they enter the building they move slowly
Toward the lift, for the fifth floor;
And once in the flat she makes his tea,
Settling him with a book for an hour or so.

Then quietly, determinedly,
She collects her music,
Closes the door gently,
And walks down the stairs
To the grand piano
In the communal lounge.

Now at last she can lift the lid, reverently,
Adjust the stool to a comfortable height,
And select an étude, a sonata or a fugue.

For a moment, holding the silence,
Her hands are poised over the keys.

Then, extravagantly,
The music bubbles and exults,
It foams, scatters and roars,
Coruscates and trembles, cascading
Entirely at her own pace.

I Feel the Flow of Your Tears

I feel the flow of your tears,
The flood of your pain;
I know the hurt
Is deeper than
This damaged leg,
This throbbing bone.
Your eyes which just now
Shone with your brilliant smile,
Are clouded with some unexplained agony.
You try to find words,
I try to find a question to help you.
We both fail.
Your glory is diminished
By this inarticulate suffering;
I long to draw the sting
And take it to myself;
But I do not know where I am;
Nor do you.

It suggests a violence witnessed long ago,
The terror of another's pain unleashed
Irrationally; a foreign anger
You do not dare to remember.
I could not help you then;
I cannot now.

Tomorrow you will smile again
And all will be forgotten,
But not healed.
And I shall want to hold you

To absorb the poison
From the wound.
Shall I still
Be so tightly bound
I cannot come near;
Or will you turn me away
With the indifference
Of your hand?

It Is I Who Speak

I receive your distinct messages,
Accept the sense patterns of my awaking;
I am being deep-dyed with your colours.
Take care, care of me.

As I absorb the nutrient elements of your being,
I am flooded with the intimate music of your moods,
The chemistry of your joys, your angers and your fears.
Be gentle, gentle with me.

I register the flavour, sounds,
The stimuli of your substance,
And shall use all as the fabric of my future.
Be aware, aware of me.

Are you waiting to influence my growth,
To mould me as you would wish me to be
Later, in the home you have prepared
For my arrival?

But this is my arrival, here,
Where your impulses resonate
Along the lifelines of my forming,
In this amniotic home.

Listen for my foetal whispers.
We are sculpting, together, now,
The structures of my inscape.
Listen. It is I who speak.

3.

*"The time is now,
It can never be again;
It is enough."*

Late Harvest

Out of the drum of my tight humming life
I see the evening feeling for the night;
Children revolve aimlessly in the street
Like snowflakes, cracking the air
With their voices; it will freeze to steel.

How unsharp I am after this time;
I have tried all orthodox ways,
Conformed until I am a stranger within myself,
Wild as a cat's eyes in cold corners.

But this is not the end;
Empty me of my desire,
Thresh me to peace.
I have tried against you.

Jigsaw

We are here,
And we have a jigsaw to do... with help.
All the pieces are there in the box –
The bright colours, the sombre, the violent,
The quiet, the disturbing, the gentle.
The edges are there, the corners, the strange shapes
That don't look as if they belong anywhere.
There is a design, but it's not revealed
On the cover of the box this time,
We shall have to find it for ourselves... with help.

No, it's not a question of changing the shapes,
Repainting the colours, throwing pieces away,
Or forcing them in where they're not meant.
We have to find the right order, the right way to use them;
To place them with determination and patience... and with
    help.

Then we shall begin, slowly,
To glimpse something of the intended design;
And in this lies the secret, and the lesson:
Determination, patience, and courage... with help.
And each piece placed reveals more of the whole work.
The mystery is that all those ugly, strangely-shaped pieces,
When you find the right place for them,
Suddenly seem to beautify and make sense
Of the whole emerging pattern.

We are here, and we have a jigsaw to do… with help.
And when, finally, we can do no more,
We know we shall not have completed the whole design,
But we shall have done much of the framework,
And fitted several useful groups together. We can begin
To sense what it's all about, and where it may be going.

The important thing is not to throw away
Any of those awkward bits… they're all part of the pattern,
They're going to be essential somewhere. You see
It's just a matter of finding the right place for them…
With help.

Prodigy

1. *for Matthew*

The child, head uplifted,
Moves white-robed facing us,
In a profound harmony
With your every gesture,
Your every sculpting of the air.
His innocence and vulnerability
Reflect, as he dances,
Your dignity,
Your energy,
Your discipline.

Behind the boy
You tell your Advent story;
Your fingers stretch
To caress the light
Arching above your head;
Your arms flow outward,
Shaping the space around you;
Then, finely, you articulate
The symmetry,
The gift,
Of your body,
As you bow earthward
In a simple submission
Towards us.

You have, together,
Measured your radiant duet
In serenity and freedom;
You have moved to the life-rhythms
In which you delight,
While your shadows,
Black-etched behind you,
Have danced the gold,
The frankincense,
The myrrh.

2. *for Michael*

Until I heard you play, your small form
Riding with delight the wave-crests
Of the music's insistent demand,
Your dance of curls dark-reflecting
The rhythms of its ebb and flow;

Until I saw you move, your child's body
Possessed by the imperative of your gift,
Your bow leaping along the line
Into the frenzy of an arpeggio;

Until I felt the impress of your life-energy
Among the cascades of harmony, knew your instrument
As the voice of your inner dedication,

I had never rejoiced in the resonance,
The storm-surge of my own silent music.

Now, as I catch the echoes
Of your freedom and exhilaration,

You are leading me on your jubilant journey,
Released from all restraints
Of distant doubt and future sorrow;
You are focusing all my hunger
In the holiness of the moment,
As the orchestra lifts you
Towards the wild-fire of the cadenza;

You plunge into the climactic thunder,
The ecstasy of the coda,
Then thrust your bow upward
High above your head
In a triumphant impulse of celebration.

Your colours are as fragrance,
Your sound an exultation;
The time is now,
It can never be again;
It is enough.

Watchman

Suggested by Habakkuk 2

I am the sightless watchman
And I stand upon my tower;
I sense the children growing,
Changing, growing, hour by hour.
I sense Time's wind is blowing.
Rivers of people flowing.
I sense the people flowing
In Time's relentless power.
　　I sense the people passing,
　　On and on, and always passing;
　　I am the sightless watchman
　　And I stand upon my tower.

I am the sightless watchman
And I grip my leaning wall;
I hear the people stumbling.
I hear the people fall;
I hear the houses crumbling.
The solid buildings crumbling.
The mighty buildings tumbling;
A mother's urgent call.
　　I hear the people passing
　　On and on, and always passing;
　　I am the sightless watchman
　　And I grip my leaning wall.

I am the sightless watchman
In my agony of mind;
I feel the folk regretting
The waste they've left behind,
And never yet forgetting,
Now that their day is setting,
I feel the folk regretting
All they will never find.
  I feel the people passing
  On and on, and always passing,
  I am the sightless watchman
  In my agony of mind.

I am the sightless watchman
Standing upon my height;
The stream of folk unending
Passes beyond the light.
Time's mastery unbending
The old and young is sending,
The great and weak is sending
Along into the night.
  I see the people passing
  On and on, and always passing;
  I am the sightless watchman;
  But I pass into the night.

Only Good People Kill Themselves

Forgive me if I'm wrong,
But I thought priests
Were not supposed
To contemplate suicide.

They have, after all,
Their God,
And their God tells them
That he will help them
Counter the dark impulses
That invade our consciousness,
So often without apparent reason.
And besides – it's wrong;
He gave us life
And we shouldn't even think
Of throwing it back.

But what happens
When the inner dictates
Obscure all reason,
And what is more,
All faith?

To a simpler
Less committed person
There would always be
A way out;
He could share the blame,
Or thrust it all on others.

But that is not for you,
Now shut in your room
With no razor,
Supervised hour by hour,
Only to have the misery
Perpetuated, when enough
Is already enough.

You have been told
Time and again
That you are not responsible
For these voices,
Amid such inexplicable
Periods of fear,
Illogical panic,
And dread of nameless,
Unfocused forces.
Yet you are determined
To remain the person
You have imagined yourself to be
All this time:
Priest, the man for God,
Pastor, the man for your flock.
Have you felt safe
Only in this determination?

And now,
Any threat or circumstance
Which might expose the gap

Between the gentle, delicate
Almost holy version of yourself
You have constructed,
And this recent eruption
Of an alien reality,
Makes surviving much longer
Unbearable.

For you are good,
And only good people
Kill themselves.
You are good because
You try to stay true
To the self
You believe yourself to be
At any cost –
Too good to blame
Any other person
For what they might
Have caused you to become.
You are unable to offer
A necessary forgiveness
Because you will not own
Any origin for your agony;
Your anger, suddenly now
Most terrible,
Is directed only at yourself.

Forgive me if I'm wrong,
But I hope
The God you have served
And worshipped devotedly
For so long,
Will ultimately
Prove to be
More charitable
Towards you,
Than you, whoever you are,
Have been able
To be.

Communion Anthem

This is my body, offered you,
A body, torn and racked with pain,
Calling you back to walk my way,
And know your finer selves again.

This is my life-blood harshly shed,
Drained to the last for care of you,
Calling you from the vain and false,
To claim the beautiful and true.

I had no other I could share,
There was no more that I could give,
Open your hands at my table here,
Come, that you may learn to live.

My feast shall fill you with my life,
My love shall hold you day by day,
You are to be my body now,
So dare to give yourselves away.

Choral Evensong

The old man watches you,
Watches you singing.
It is then his memories come,
And hints of somewhere beyond
Lift him from the darkness.
They come from long before,
And will be always, after.
The old man watches you singing,
Your every movement,
Your concentrated energy
Dedicated
To the perfection of the music.

The old man listens,
Listens to you singing.
It is then the doors of perception
Open – your icons of sound
Lead him into worlds
Only a shadow's breadth away,
And yet unknown
To those who pass, unaware.
They are there for him,
There for you; you meet
Where sound and colour,
Touch and scent
Elide, are one.
The old man listens,
Listens to you singing.

The old man sings with you,
Sings with you in his heart,

A heart you bring to life again,
A heart you lift
Into fields of fragrance
That are outside time
And beyond place,
Lift into the clearest air
Where winds flow, iridescent,
And angels call.
The old man sings with you
In his heart.

And somehow you can do this,
Somehow you can know,
Somehow you can tell him
Of a far greater beauty,
Where you share the mystery together,
The hurt and the joy,
The searching and the longing;
Where you share some of the answer
Which lies at the heart
Of the loving.
It is so,
It is ever so;
It has always been,
It will always be
So.

Transcendence

Choral Evensong, Ash Wednesday, King's College Chapel, 1997

Crystalline
Your voices
Lighten my darkness,
Ringing
Into the vaulted roof
Exquisite.

Singing still
The harmonies hang in the air
Like incense.
Now at last
Will you let me depart
In peace?

It is ended.
The glory dissolves
Into the darkness
And is silent.
Transient footsteps
Retreat
Down the nave.

But your voices
Hover
In the vault
Of my memory,
Shining.

O the tears,
The tears at the heart of things.

Agape

This is the love that holds me, still,
Despite the shifting sand;
Amid the anger, toil and fret
He shields me with his hand.

This is the love that never leaves
Despite my stubborn will;
That stays to calm, to ease, to heal,
The love that calls me still.

This is the love that crowns my life
When hurt and guilt assail,
When all I trust is broken down,
When all I try shall fail.

This is the love that knows my heart
When all I feel is shame;
Helps me to face my inner self
And calls me by my name.

It is a love that sets me free
When all around is fear;
A love that watches over me,
A love forever near.

Such a love believes in me
When all I know is doubt;
A love that always comes to me,
A love that seeks me out.

This is the love that holds me, still,
Despite the shifting sand;
Calls me to seek the higher way,
And guides me with his hand.

Greek has four words for Love: one is for family affection; one for companionship and friendship; one for physical love; and the fourth (agapē) is the word used, particularly in the New Testament, for the self-giving, unconditional love that seeks only and always the good of the loved one.

Puer Nobis Natus Est

Accused one,
There was no language
For you to communicate
Your inner life,
Your vibrant, fertile spirit,
Comprehending us all.

You gave us only images,
Stories that might connect
With our inner truths.
But our truths were obscured
And diminished in us;
They would have allowed you
No way through.

So we sent you
To your new beginning,
Executed one,
Leaving you
Only one word
To offer us;
And that was concealed
In your total submission
To our freedom.

Puer nobis natus,
Let us interpret this word
In passion and audacity,
If we have ears to hear.

Puer absconditus,
After the wintering of the soul,
Comes to us
Renaissance of possibility.

Of course, you are dangerous,
Disturbing, unpredictable;
You would keep us
Always moving,
Moving, aspiring;
You do not offer us
Safety or stability;
Yet in you we find
Renewed vitality,
Purpose and potential;
In you the spirit soars.

Puer absconditus,
Innate, profound
Playfulness, creativity
Of wisdom and folly;
Puer nobis natus,
Spirit of youth and radiance,
Essence of new beginning,
Fresh turning of the wheel.

4.

"Plead
For us, who destroy in others' beauty
Our godly image and human likeness"

Dren's Song

Kosovo, 1999

I am Dren Caka,
And they only got me
In the arm.
But it hurt and I screamed
When they cut off my shirt
And dressed the wound
On that table there.
I was not as brave
As I thought,
It seems.

I am Dren Caka,
The last of my line.
They came where we were hiding,
Twelve of us in the cellar,
Trapped with no protection,
Clinging to each other there.
Being ten years old
Does not exempt you
Nowadays,
It seems.

I am Dren Caka,
Pretending I was dead,
Not a sound or a movement there;
Too many, far too many
Bullets to escape.
But they only got me in the arm,

In the centre
Of the huddle.
I was lucky,
It seems.

I am Dren Caka,
Ten years old,
Fed and watered, cleaned and sheltered,
Trying to rest on this bed
In the half-light.
But now I am beginning
To remember,
And I do not dare to sleep,
For who will protect me here
From my dreams?

Water Rats

After a late Victorian photograph by Frank Meadow Sutcliffe

Morning,
Before the full power
Of a June sky;
The harbour still cooled
By the prevailing
North Sea breeze;
And there the idle
Whitby coble
Besieged
By a riot of children
'In puris naturalibus',
As you said.

Sea urchins,
Small bodies bright
With sun and sea-soak,
A leaping, writhing,
Splashing gambol
Of life and uproar.

And so you came
On your familiar
Diurnal round,
And with your rapid
Artist's eye,
To seize that instant,
Hold it
On the heavy glass negative
Of your cumbersome camera.

When, later, you refined
Your prints,
You chose those soft
And subtle sepia tones
To enhance
The essence of light and lightness,
The aesthetic quality
Of the scene's inscape.

Then the exhibitions,
And the praise,
The Prince requesting
An enlarged copy
For Marlborough House.

And then the opprobrium,
The harsh words,
The half-formed assumptions,
The excommunication
By local clergy,
The stolid bigotry
Of the righteous.

And what of the bright boys
Who, twenty years later,
Were sent by the righteous
To writhe
With the trench rats,

Their sleet-soaked bodies
Held
Under the full power
Of a December sky –
Essence of light denied?

It was to be
A different kind
Of uproar, riot, gamble,
I hear.
And we have been unearthing
Their boots, and their badges,
Their buckles, and their bones,
For the last seventy years.

An Unsentimental Epitaph for Stephen Baltz Aged Eleven

Boeing crash, New York, 18 December 1960

I expect like most boys one sees on asphalt playgrounds
You have played with planes of your own construction,
Holding them high, and making them dip and dive
As you commanded; and forcing explosive noises
Out of the sides of your mouth
Where now your blood shows.

Such activities of course had no particular object
Beyond your own amusement and the passing of time;
While ours have more serious purposes,
Being, I suppose, to increase the general efficiency
And convenience of life
To an ultimate.

But you reached your ultimate a little early,
Flung lung-scorched and red head blackened
To get a death
As pointless
As my anger.

Requiem for Jody

Jody Dobrowski – kicked to death October 2005 aged 24

Put on the purple now and weep
For all the gentle of the Earth;
Put on the purple now and mourn
The meek we use to purge our rage.
Take him, grave, for cherishing –
Miserere Domine.

Put on the purple now and grieve;
Once this was a spirit's dwelling
By the breath of God created,
High the heart that here was beating;
Broken beyond all mortal semblance,
Symbol now of love distorted.
Take him, grave, for cherishing –
Et in paradisum, angeli.

Put on the purple and lament;
Earth, with fragrant petals scattered,
Take him now for cherishing;
On your tender breast receive him
Noble in his disfigurement –
Aeternam habeat requiem.

Take him, grave, for cherishing,
Guard him well, the dead we give you.
Put on the white again and pray
For those we harm in love denied;
Put on the white again and pray
The fury we cannot own or forgive;

Put on the white to kneel and plead
For us, who destroy in others' beauty
Our godly image and human likeness –
De profundis Domine.

Dark Victory

So now do I see the road ahead
With no small hand in mine,
Knowing you must sleep in your own dark bed
With no bright star to shine.

Now do I see the desert track
With no bright look of love,
Only the wild and wind-swept wrack,
And a winter sky above.

Now do I summon all my strength
To face a journey long,
To take the steps, the length on length,
But no soft voice of song.

And you must live, and yet be dead,
And I must walk and weep,
'Tis best that nothing now be said
To call you from your sleep.

Lamentation of the Unnamed Boy

I am unnamed, I have no name,
Unless it be rage. Shall rage be my name?
I wanted to shout my unspoken word,
To part the trophies of his birthday trainers
And his pocket money among the others,
But it wasn't enough, for rage is my name.

It wasn't enough, for rage is my name;
I destroyed in him the disfigured me.
I don't plead affliction or register sorrows
To purge my primal lamentation;
Though grief is my name, forsaken my name,
Names are just words, and words have no meaning.

Names are just words, and words have no meaning.
Let rage be my name, for today I spoke
With the bricks that hammered, the knife that pierced;
I spoke out clearly my ten-year-old Passion
On his ten-year-old body, foetal, stricken;
But I could not destroy the word on his face.

I could not destroy the word on his face;
And for legal reasons I cannot be named.
I was dumb before them, having no answer,
So, shrouded beneath the policeman's blanket,
I am unnamed, I have no name,
Unless it be rage. Shall rage be my name?

Mass of the Day for Whichever Unknown Saint Will Take On the Patronage of the Abnormal

KYRIE

First of all, of course I cry mercy
But to whom, to whom then?
Could you be prepared to speak for me,
Not because you will be rewarded,
Or because you are curious to analyse
Deviant compulsions,
But because you recognise readily in yourself,
Even now, a disturbing fallibility,
And still, yourself, ask for mercy.
Are you going to be there for me, crying
Kyrie eleison, Kyrie eleison?

GLORIA

It will not be easy for you,
It will be threatening certainly
To your previously formed assumptions
About normal behaviour,
Because I cry glory to a beauty
You do not see through my eyes.
I perceive this beauty
With an intensity channelled
Through an aberrant chemistry,
Which you probably believe
Is now rigidly programmed –
Intractable machine.
Yet it was gifted to me
Personally and purposefully.
Gloria in excelsis.

CREDO

And I have to believe
In reason and purpose.
This may be folly,
But it is not fortuitous.
It has taken more than half a life
To register and accept
Who I am, how I was to be.
And I have to take this with me,
Find the holy within it;
For if I reject
I shall not find my purpose,
Or my reason – my reason
In some far wider purpose.
There's no alternative
To this credo.

SANCTUS

Sanctus. Sanctus,
Yes, do not be surprised,
I believe in the holy,
And reach for it in the beauty,
For the beauty in the innocence.
And since to sanctify means
To make holy,
I have to turn to a source of perfection,
With which I hope you are in contact,
To help me achieve this
Sacrificially.
Will you be there
Because of your comparative imperfection,
Or have you reached a too distant and remote
Sanctity and blessedness?

BENEDICTUS

Blessèd is he who is born
Into the holiness of welcome and sacrifice;
Blessèd is he who is reared
In the sanctity of wisdom and faithfulness.
Hallowed place.
Benedictus. Benedictus.

Blessèd is he who comes
With few destabilising impulses;
Blessèd is he who grows
In wonder and reverence for all that is in being.
Blessèd indeed.
Benedictus. Benedictus.

AGNUS DEI

And blessèd are you, holy one,
If you can find it in your spiritual fibres
To reach out to any who might
Take the vulnerable lamb
To drink forcibly at its innocence,
Destroying the glory,
Blaspheming the sacred.
Blessèd are you if you can do this,
And cry, yourself, for mercy:
Agnus Dei
Qui tollis peccata mundi,
Dona nobis pacem.

Are you going to be there for me?

Charley Dies

for the young people who came

When the priest proclaimed,
'Blesséd are they who mourn
For they shall be comforted',
Was it really any consolation
To know that comforted
Means strengthened?
Does the Creator
Send suffering like this
Deliberately
To make us strong
And blesséd?

I suppose helplessness and hurt
Can teach us something,
Though others outside us
May never know exactly what,
Because it happens
At the deepest place,
Where we come face to face
With who we really are,
At the point of growth;
If we ever dare approach
Such a holy place.

We shall not be able to answer
Why this has happened like this,
Nor why Charley lay there
Passively, all those weeks.

But she was not lying there
Distanced from us;
She was speaking to us
In her silence,
Saying many things
To each of us in different ways,
Some frightening, some painful,
And always challenging.

Takes courage, compassion,
Faithfulness and character
For young people to face
The bewildering, threatening
Technology of an ITU,
The impersonal, clinical environment
Of a general ward.

Yet you came, always,
You kept coming.
And did you know
You had such qualities,
Such resources,
Before Charley called them
From you?
It was always tough,
It probably made you angry
To see her like that;
Yet you still couldn't help
Doing it for her
In the best way you knew.

Of course pain can always
Be deadened,
If you turn away,
Shut yourself off,
Try to pretend
It's not happening.
But the only way out
Is always, and only,
The way
Straight through the middle.

And what of her parents' pain,
The pain of all her family?
What of that, above all else?
Their love for her always drew them
To receive the hurt,
And also the consolation –
That bitter mixture –
Accepted by being with her.

Even her death was not as fearful
As we had dreaded;
For we, each of us, experienced
A sense of abiding stillness,
Of completion,
A reassurance that filled her room
As we came to say goodbye.

Charley in her helplessness,
Charley in her passivity,
Has given much to us
Over these months.

Some of it we may know already,
More we shall know, and thank her for
In time to come.

To be sure we shall not forget,
To be sure we shall not be the same
As if we had never come;
For she has spoken to us
Across the barriers of ourselves,
Spoken to us in her stillness,
All this long while of our coming.

Above all else in life
We are given each other.
Everything Charley gave to you,
And called from you,
Was important.
Do not regret it;
Do not waste it.

Never expect to find easy answers.
But you can find meaning;
And you will find it only
In your own stillness,
At the centre of the pain,
In the secret chamber of your being –
The place of growth,
The place of blessing.

Blesséd are they who mourn,
For they shall be comforted.

Terminal Care Ward

It shall be jolted from me
Not permitted to sneak
From between
Your tidied hospital sheets
Taking all its time
While these others watch on,
Sideways looking, most from their backs,
Awkwardly.

I know the drill,
For I've watched them watching others
Before me;
And I've found myself at it often enough.
It must be struck out of me.

'Don't hold and hinder,
Let me get at the brooms and barrow in the sheds.'

Narrow it along the side-path by the greenhouses,
Sparrows coming at you for toast crumbs from breakfast,
Scatter.

'It does matter.
I shall not drink
Your pale ward tea
Even for you.
It never is the same
As my yellow pot makes.
I'm tired of the taste;
Yes, it matters.'

Scatter and return to the yard
With the spattering of rain;
Panes cracked, tiles loosened,
The council sheds padlocked.
It was half-past seven when I came by the tower,
Now it's well after time I picked out the tackle
And moved.

'Mr Williams, the sheds are locked sir,
Time I was moving.'

The showers will help to keep the dust down,
It blows up so when the cars cut close to the edge;
And the air currents knock you
And dart their particles against your hands and eyelids;
Great articulated diesels pulsating as they pass,
Shoving the heatwave into you…

'Yes I'll be clearing the rust from the handle shafts
A day or two soon, sir'

It's getting old like me.

'I'm not so old that I need always helping down
Thank you; if you will reach me my slippers,
I can manage the rest.
I am not so old as you think;
Not as old
As I look.'

Look,
'Look, my stretch of road for this morning'

The by-pass is in full flood of day
With the flare of windscreens;
They speed windscreaming by.

'Don't hold me, don't hold me.'

My dreg of life is not to be filtered off
Strictly under supervision;
They alone, with their irresistible strength,
Shall strike it out of me.

Bomb Site

Child, you show me
The long scar jagging
Across your abdomen;
Your fingerless left hand.
You reveal to me
Your collateral damage;
It is over, part of you,
Accepted;
No questions asked.

Child, your mother's embrace
Could not save you;
Her protective flesh
Fused into yours
By the inferno of impact;
And your deaths
Fused with a thousand others.
You had no chance
To form your question;
Now it is over,
Accepted.

Child, the kind, detached man
Came and asked you –
As you lay upon
The fracturing earth,
Your belly bloated
To a phantom sufficiency –
Did you really mean it
When you said
You wanted death to come
Rapidly?

You are only eight
And have no question;
It is part of you,
Accepted.

Child, the men came,
While you hid under your covers,
And threw you
Upon the stone floor.
They crushed your thigh bones
With the butts
Of their rifles
To teach your father his lesson,
And left you
Unable to find a question
In the central fireball
Of such pain.
It is over, part of you,
Accepted.

You are calling to us, each
In your voiceless Passion;
And we must articulate
Now
Your necessary question.

5.

*"From the vortex of spiralling void at centre
I reach for you."*

Song Sequence

'No matter how old we are, we still have time to let the light in, to break down the barriers we once erected between us and our truest self. Nothing is so sad as regretting our unlived lives, our untold stories, our unsung songs. Yet, in God's extravagance, during our last times, everything lost – the dream, the innocence, the melody – can all be restored.'

Adapted from 'Home Before Dark' by Daniel O'Leary

1. PRELUDE

I shall make a ring richer than all,
For my perfect joy now, and for time
That is coming;
I shall take the diamond air
From the white velvet
Of a winter morning;
The moon pearl
From the black velvet
Of a winter evening,
And set them
In the fashioned gold of my singing,
To make a ring richer than all.

2. AUBADE ONE

It was, of all places, in Jubilee Street,
One of the grey roads backing onto the sidings,
At the time they illuminate their little front rooms
And you can catch a glimpse of the interiors
Before they are quick-curtained from you.
It was there, and only for a moment,
That I best knew myself.

In one of the many parlours that open straight upon the
    pavement,
They had a piano cumbered with thick china vases,
And photographs in thinning silver frames.
I knew it to be dusted, but never played,
Polished, but long since untuned; that it had
A redolence of moth-balls put in too late,
The lid fast down, the keys yellowing in darkness.

3. CHACONNE

Now when time's measure promised nothing more
But retribution and the tang of shame,
The sourish scrapings of the storehouse floor,
Proper reward for having failed the game;

Now while I waited my dessert of lees
Resignedly, and as my due and right,
At mid-point of my journey, expecting no release
From stumbling down the crumbling edge of night;

You curled, sleeping, beside me on the lurching coach's seat,
Your head upon my lap, your cheek against my hand;
Diffusion of your entity through mine, radiant, complete,
And the wheat swaying and abounding from the land.

We returned from swimming, my hand, on the fragility of
    your shoulder,
Discerned beneath its slender rhythm the firm bone;
All this I must keep, before we grow both older,
And each is to be separate and alone.

You take me down the orchard to the lopped branches
    burning,
I watch the delicate proportion of your limbs,
The way you stand, absorbed into yourself, and turning,
Confront the violent movement of the flames.

4. AUBADE TWO

For your voice is clear
With the waking tear,

Your skin as clear
As the flower of the pear,

You are sweet and fresh
In the ripening flesh;

We must seek the seed of our richest store
Deep within the bitter core.

5. SERENATA

You come in the night's velvet hollow,
Brown eyes to follow me, open lips to draw me.

You come in soft darkness to hold me,
Your body enfold me, your energy know me.

This delight I could not choose,
Nor your bright comfort lose as you calm me.

Not in time, nor in place,
You bring the way of grace to affirm me.

6. SARABANDE ONE

When I consider how much pain has gone
To make me as I am, and this is all I am,
I think that what's to come must now be nearly done,
And with the few short pleasures, all the blame;

The blame and every effort of pretence
With which I fix my hours in rigid cast,
Ruthlessly censor the product of each sense,
Living with what is left in solitary fast.

And then I turn to alleviate my fear,
Finding the level where we both can meet;
Nothing gives comfort but your presence here,
Enough to watch you simply, simply to feel you greet
Me with the eager lifting of your eye;
By this my basest ore you purify.

7. SARABANDE TWO

I would not ask your love, though longing,
But only what you offer take;
However strong the feelings thronging,
Submit to you for beauty's sake.

I would not take your love, though needed,
But only what you freely give;
My inner movement held, unheeded,
Friendship remain, delight survive.

I would not ask your love, though aching,
To lose the glory most I fear;
Love must grow free, it's not for making,
I only hold what you offer here.

Occasions change and moments vanish,
Evenings of innocence remove;
No act of mine shall heartsease banish,
Bruise the fragility of love.

I will not demand, though heart be breaking,
Will not stretch out to grasp so much;
Your love is here and now awaking
To heal with the colours of your touch.

8. CANZONETTA ONE

And is that smile
The key you have for me
To unlock the treasures of your innocence,
The perfumes of your freedom,
My privilege to see?

And do you know that I am
Seeking you with my soul's perception,
Do you know that I am reaching for you,
Your head unturned the while?

For we are drawn into that momentary
And infinite miracle
When your smile liberates me,
Opening the gate upon the scented meadows
And the jewelled air of your bright dominion.

9. CANZONETTA TWO

To focus you now as you are,
Before the glass flaws or cracks,
Before my concentration on you
Burns out to a white smoking point
And blackens, or the eye
Cataracts.

Time floods through us
Dragging each particle on;
Holding against the wind,
Momentarily,
We hover, parallel.
But we shall be snatched away
From now, and
From each other.

A fly drops on its back,
Entwining its legs in spinning anger
After a short day.

I focus the modulation of your voice,
The half-spoken word at your lip,
While the camellia's waxen petals
Rust at the tip.

10. ETUDE ONE

You come with your touch to enchant me,
You come on my breast to lie;
You come with your kiss to delight me,
A shadow passing by.

As yestertime you enthral me,
And break my heart with your smile,
You come with your halo of brightness
To stay with me just for a while.

You come with your beauty to win me,
To breathe on my cheek with your sigh,
You move through my soul to restore me,
A shadow passing by.

11. ETUDE TWO

Should death curtail my register of days,
Will you remember some of all our ways;
This fragment of our lives that we have shared,
The moments held in mystery, the moments dared?

Will you remember some, as life moves on,
You to develop, I to absorb, what's gone;
Your life-enhancing presence near to mine
Releasing what endures, to strengthen and refine?

You may not know all you have given me:
Calming the pains that long have driven me,
Consolidating tenderness, concern,
New ways of offering my life to learn;

But will you remember this, as days go by,
How deeply in my arms you'd come to lie;
How comfort, strength would flow from you to me,
From me to you, a healing energy?

Some of myself shall live as part of you,
And gentleness and sacrifice renew;
So then give thanks – for this, of all our ways,
When death curtails my register of days.

12. TOCCATA ONE

How did you know me sheathed in my disguise,
By what rare alchemy or arcane power;
How pierced you straight my barricades of lies
By calling to me from your silver tower?

All comes together now, you bid the fake
Retrieve himself in you and cure his ills;
The ceaseless dragging of a teasing ache
Is quite annulled. So the vacuum fills

And I return, beyond where I was sold,
The treacherous years when I was forced to hurl
Into a smelting pit of steel my dreams of gold,
To where you call me from your turret room of pearl.

13. TOCCATA TWO

In laughter's wild kaleidoscope,
Its patterned gifts of joy and hope,
We taste the light, we seize the height,
Alone each other see.

Fanfares of fragrance and colour enhance
Our riotous cadenza, our sun-gilt dance,
Out of all time to lift and climb,
Alone for each other be.

This will not last, it cannot stay,
We take it now, if later pay;
So much will fade, our strength decayed,
But my life has touched yours this brief day.

14. IMPROMPTU

The steel seethed and is cold,
We are old.

We could not hold the dancers' leap,
The wonder keep.

We may have gift again;
But then must sleep.

15. THRENODY ONE

Texture of my living torn from me,
Unravelling, fragmenting my cohesion,
From the vortex of spiralling void at centre
I reach for you.

Your hand has held
The rich hope of summer afternoons;
Your eye has held
The pastel tones of an evening welcome;
We must guard the silken flame
Which stands serene
Against the intensity of darkness;
Sacred point
In the cataleptic night
Surrounding us.

16. THRENODY TWO

You, Easter lily,
Stand close in our sanctuary,
Immaculate.

All the while I called to you,
I spoke your name,
Your name again.

Stand close in our sanctuary.

We retreat into the fastness,
The still colour
Below the pulse of speech,
To the cool place of shadow.

Stand close in our sanctuary,
Immaculate.

All the while I called to you,
I called your name, your name again,
All the while I spoke to you,
Allaying the pain in some measure.

17. THRENODY THREE

Excised
Beyond the range of your calling,
I am hooded in night.
A glacial dark sweeps through me,
Impermeable,
Turbulent limbo.

And I go through the motions,
Through the motions,
Motions merely;
I go through the motions of living
Merely.

18. THRENODY FOUR

This is the way outward, the only way,
Through the stale, the whining night,
Keeping the brightness in the inner room
Velvet curtained. I am far from summer.

This is the way outward, the only way,
Held by the steel track, the blind tunnel;
My time is drying.
The wind is shredding the light,
The blackened sunflower lowers its head;
My strength is flaking off.

This is the way outward, the only way,
Through the stale, the whining night,
Keeping the brightness in the inner room
Velvet curtained. I am far from summer.

19. ARABESQUE

Kiss me with the kisses of your mouth,
For your love is richer than wine;
Your lips drop as the honeycomb,
Honey and milk are under your tongue;
The fragrance of your body
Is like the oils and spices of Lebanon.

I have made the light
Shimmer on your opening lips
With my finger's touch;
With my finger's touch
I have traced
The supple perfection of your limbs,
The opalescence of your cheek,
The golden down of your thigh;
My lips have rested
In the close, soft bowl of your palm,
In the velvet recess of your eyelids.

Without you I was nothing
In the dimension of time,
Nowhere in the dimension of space,
As I had been
Before you called me
From a random oblivion
In the desert alleyways
Of the turbulent galaxies;
Distilled me into being
In the rich harmonic,

The vibrant landscapes,
Of your joyous universe.

My senses have explored the symmetry,
The texture and the perfume of your substance;
Behold, your head is filled with dew,
Your locks with the droplets of the night;
Set me as a seal upon your heart,
Set me as a seal upon your arm;
For many waters cannot quench love,
Neither can the floods overwhelm it.

I look to a place beyond desire
To which the hungry of soul aspire;
Look to a time far distant hence
Born of a keen benevolence.

In a time beyond time, a place beyond place,
Where we dare reveal our naked face,
Nurtured in trust and reverence,
We may welcome the challenge of difference.

Long after the years now left to me,
I sense a generous charity
Whose healed perception, no more spent
In partial law's sere continent,
Shall read the deeper soul's intent.

For there, beyond the rigid state
Of prejudice and custom's weight,
Mirage and shadow shall dissipate,
And every action, word and wound
At last in love's judgement shall be found,
And with life's radiance abound.

We spoke across the walls of time
A language never taught,
Come from our essence, hallowed place,
Singing from heart to heart.

We spoke through eye and touch and breath,
We reached to take and bind;
A calm transcendence filled our life
Calling from mind to mind.

We spoke beyond the weight of things
Transforming, making whole;
Infinite fields of our childhood's delight
We knew from soul to soul.

22. ARIETTA TWO

Singing across the fifty years
Your word of promise
Comes to me,
Silver-shining.

It recalls the purity and expectation,
The ease and energy
Of your voice's movement,
Carefree in its range and freedom.

Now is your body lost,
Perhaps in frailty, probably in decay;
But the melody is recaptured
In mind and heart.

With a longing and a reverence
For the Composer's intention,
I hear surely, distinctly,
Your soul song calling me
Into our distant pilgrimage.

23. ELEGY

My soul held silent within me
In awe and still delight.
I waited for you to smile
From the soft brownness
Of your gentle eyes,
Your brown, gentle eyes
Smiling.
Swan of joy and ease
On the ebony pool of my night.

I welcomed the summer's humming days,
The touch of dancing lilac on the eye.
I lived in the chant of floating smoke,
Felt the harp's caress
Echoing down a silken wind.
I found my ease
In the musk of shadows,
In the oboe theme.

Frail, tiny, paper boat
Launched upon mountainous seas;
Delicate butterfly wings in a harsh wind;
Honeysuckle fragrance of a late summer evening,
Intense, transient, vulnerable.

O taste and see that the Lord is good;
How sweet are His words upon my tongue.
Through the benediction of your nearness,
The incense of your affection,
You have been His word of love
Spoken to me.

24. CAVATINA

I wait upon your footsteps' fall
To free the stifled voice's call,
I wait upon your opening hand
With heart's intent to understand;
I crouch beside the dying heat
As strengths of mind and limb retreat,
Hold and endure the solemn wake
Lest the dark caller overtake.

But would you turn and then ignore
This hand upon the long-barred door,
Never know the unbound word
And breath of welcome overheard?
If my spent heart could wake its beat,
Stir to the spring of urgent feet,
We might, now strangers, cross these years;
But oh the tears, the tears, the tears.

25. BERCEUSE

The cadence of your evening song
Still echoes sweet and clear
Along the corridors of pain
And down the aching year.

Though you've passed beyond my reaching
My senses hold you yet,
And in the ring of memory
Your brilliant diamonds set.

So eager then your smile for me,
So radiantly you came;
I still can see you running,
And hear you call my name.

Now, as my evening gathers,
The dancing of your laugh,
The inner jewel of your word
Shall be my epitaph.

The cadence of your evening song
Still echoes sweet and clear
Along the corridors of pain
And down the aching year.

26. NOCTURNE

Weep not aloud for innocence removed,
The unquestioned offering, acceptance proved;
Keep close in harmony the shining flame,
The urgent word, intimacy of name.

Keep close in memory the eyes as bright
Which once had brought to you alone their light;
Weep not the days by beauty led,
Keep, keep in memory the words you said.

Rejoice, rejoice love's freely offered gift,
Howe'er it came before the lurch and shift
Of circumstance and time and place;
Love's eager and accepting face.

Weep not aloud the glory that is fled,
The hands, the lips you touched, which now are dead;
Weep not aloud for moments that are gone
But keep them in delight and sing their song.